THE UNIVERSE

GALAXIES

ABDO
Publishing Company

A Buddy Book **by Marcia Zappa**

Buddy BOOKS
The Universe

VISIT US AT
www.abdopublishing.com

Published by ABDO Publishing Company, 8000 West 78th Street, Edina, Minnesota 55439.

Printed in the United States of America, North Mankato, Minnesota.
102010
012011

 PRINTED ON RECYCLED PAPER

Coordinating Series Editor: Rochelle Baltzer
Contributing Editors: Megan M. Gunderson, BreAnn Rumsch, Sarah Tieck
Graphic Design: Maria Hosley
Cover Photograph: *NASA*: MSFC.
Interior Photographs/Illustrations: *AP Photo* (p. 25); *iStockphoto*: ©iStockphoto.com/shauni (p. 28); *NASA*: ESA/S. Beckwith (STSci) and The HUDF Team (p. 27), HQ GRIN (p. 21), JPL (pp. 5, 7, 13, 17, 19, 22), JPL-Caltech (p. 9), JPL-Caltech/STSci-ESA (p. 23), JPL-Caltech, Susan Stolovy et al. (p. 11), JPL-Caltech/UCLA (p. 30), JSC-ES&IA (p. 28), MSFC (pp. 19, 29); *Photo Researchers, Inc.*: David A. Hardy (p. 15).

Library of Congress Cataloging-in-Publication Data

Zappa, Marcia, 1985-
 Galaxies / Marcia Zappa.
   p. cm. -- (The universe)
 ISBN 978-1-61714-689-3
 1. Galaxies--Juvenile literature. I. Title.
 QB857.3.Z37 2011
 523.1'12--dc22
                                      2010028582

Table Of Contents

What Is a Galaxy?

At night, tiny lights dot the sky. These are stars. In space, groups of stars form galaxies.

Galaxies come in many shapes and sizes. No one knows how many exist. Scientists say there could be more than 100 billion!

Faraway galaxies are viewed with powerful telescopes. They are interesting and beautiful sights.

A Closer Look

Besides stars, galaxies contain dust and gas. Scientists believe galaxies also have unknown stuff called dark matter. A galaxy's dark matter probably reaches far beyond the parts we see.

Galaxies are held together in space by **gravity**. Scientists think most large galaxies have a black hole in the center. This is an area of space with very strong gravity.

The pull of gravity in a black hole is so strong that it traps light! This makes it impossible to see black holes. So, scientists and artists imagine what they might look like.

The Milky Way

Earth and our sun belong to the Milky Way galaxy. Our sun is just one star in the Milky Way. Scientists believe this system contains several hundred billion stars!

Scientists think there is a huge black hole in the Milky Way's center. They say it has about 4 million times as much matter as our sun!

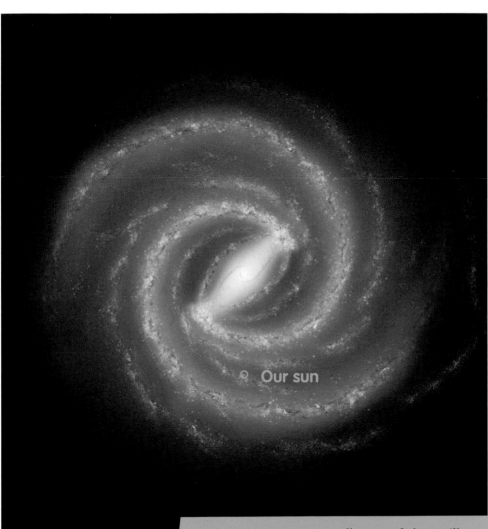

Our sun

Our sun is a very small part of the Milky Way.

Big and Small

Galaxies come in many different sizes. Some have only 100,000 stars. Others have a trillion!

In space, distance is measured in light-years. One light-year is how far light would travel in one year. This is nearly 6 trillion miles (10 trillion km)!

A small galaxy may be only a few thousand light-years across. A large galaxy may be more than 1 million light-years across! The Milky Way is about 100,000 light-years across.

The center of the Milky Way (*above*) is about 26,000 light-years from Earth.

Different Shapes

Scientists group galaxies based on their shape. The main kinds are spiral, elliptical, and irregular.

Spiral galaxies are shaped like thin disks with sweeping arms. These arms circle around the galaxy's center. Spiral galaxies have many young stars.

Most spiral galaxies have a big, ball-shaped group of stars in the center. It is called a bulge. A bulge may reach above and below the disk.

Elliptical galaxies are shaped like stretched-out balls. They are brightest at their centers. Some of the largest galaxies are elliptical. But, there are also small ones. These galaxies have many old stars.

Irregular galaxies have no certain shape. They are some of the smallest galaxies. Many new stars form in them.

Elliptical Galaxy

Spiral Galaxy

Irregular Galaxy

15

All Together Now

Most galaxies are not alone. They are part of groups, clusters, and superclusters.

A group contains fewer than 100 galaxies. Groups of galaxies form clusters. A cluster contains hundreds to thousands of galaxies.

Superclusters are made up of groups and clusters. Superclusters are huge! They are hundreds of millions of light-years across.

The closest cluster to Earth is the Virgo Cluster. It contains more than 2,000 galaxies.

Circling the Center

Stars **orbit** the center of a galaxy. Their paths give the galaxy its shape. Older, dying stars are usually near the center.

Galaxies have orbits, too. Galaxies in a group or cluster all move around the same center of **gravity**.

Stars in a spiral galaxy move in the same direction. But, they do not all move at the same speed.

19

A Galaxy Is Born

   Scientists believe galaxies started forming about 14 billion years ago! They don't know for sure how this happened. But, they have many ideas.

   Galaxies have changed over time. Scientists believe that long ago, most galaxies were small and irregular. And, they actively formed new stars.

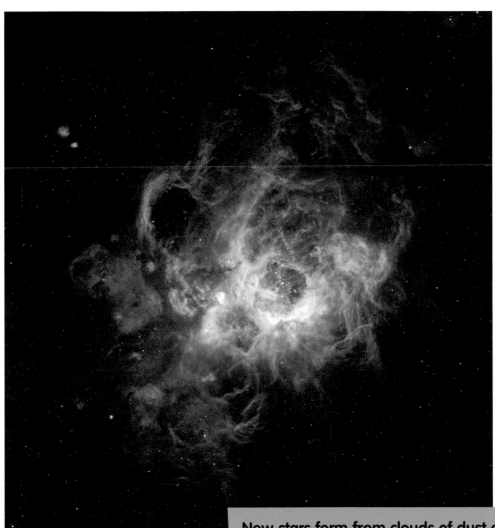

New stars form from clouds of dust and gas called nebulas (NEH-byuh-luhs).

Scientists believe that today's galaxies formed from smaller ones. Over time, galaxies can crash into each other and join together. They form new galaxies of different shapes and sizes.

Galaxy crashes are less common today than they were long ago.

Galaxy crashes create large amounts of heat and light.

Discovering Galaxies

Scientists have studied stars for thousands of years. Over time, **telescopes** and other tools helped them make discoveries.

British scientist William Herschel built his own telescopes. In the late 1700s, he used them to map the Milky Way's stars.

In the 1920s, American scientist Edwin Hubble made a discovery. He proved there are galaxies outside the Milky Way. More recently, scientists have found galaxies almost 13 billion light-years away!

Edwin Hubble was one of the first scientists to sort galaxies by shape.

Exploring Galaxies

Today, powerful **telescopes** tell scientists about galaxies. Some even **orbit** in space. They take clear pictures of faraway space objects.

The Hubble Space Telescope is based in space. It was named after Edwin Hubble. It was sent into orbit in 1990.

A Hubble Ultra Deep Field image shows almost 10,000 galaxies!

Fact Trek

Most galaxies are thousands of light-years away. When scientists view them, they see how the galaxies looked long ago. That's because their light takes so long to reach us!

Studying faraway galaxies teaches scientists about the history of outer space.

The word *galaxy* comes from the Greek word for milk.

The Milky Way is named for its appearance. Many people believe it looks like a milky stripe across the sky.

The space between galaxies is called intergalactic space. It is nearly empty.

The Andromeda galaxy is the closest large galaxy to the Milky Way. These two galaxies are moving toward each other at about 300,000 miles (500,000 km) per hour.

Andromeda (*right*) and the Milky Way could someday join. Scientists believe that in a few billion years they will form one big elliptical galaxy.

29

Voyage to Tomorrow

Scientists continue to learn about galaxies. In 2009, the WISE **telescope** was sent to space. It views young, faraway galaxies. Scientists hope it will tell them more about how galaxies were formed.

Scientists believe WISE will view some of the brightest galaxies known.

Important Words

gravity a natural force that pulls toward the center of a space object. It also pulls space objects toward each other.

orbit the path of a space object as it moves around another space object. To orbit is to follow this path.

telescope a tool used for viewing faraway objects, such as stars.

Web Sites

To learn more about **galaxies**, visit ABDO Publishing Company online. Web sites about **galaxies** are featured on our Book Links page. These links are routinely monitored and updated to provide the most current information available

www.abdopublishing.com

INDEX